Copyright © by Sandra Bacon

All rights reserved. No part of this publication may be reproduced, distributed, or transmitted
in any form or by any means, including photocopying, recording, or other electronic or mechanical methods, without the prior written permission of the publisher, except in the case of brief quotations embodied in critical reviews and certain other noncommercial uses permitted by copyright law.

www.ingramcontent.com/pod-product-compliance
Lightning Source LLC
Chambersburg PA
CBHW081654220526
45466CB00009B/2757